debt by insanity

stop the madness
there is a way to become debt free
& save money

in·san·it·y: *doing the same things over and over again and expecting different results*

I wish that I could tell you that The Secret to becoming debt free is to simply manifest it and the universe will answer. This is simply not going to happen.

If you want to become debt free and have savings, then you have to begin the transformation process.

You have to stop doing the same things over and over again.

The process begins by you making the right choices.

Only then will you begin to feel financial security and feel the stress being lifted.

If you are prepared to put in the blood, sweat and tears, then the reward at the end of the tunnel will be truly amazing.

Stop the Madness ...

TRANSFORMATION PROCESS

Lifestyle

Behavior

Sacrifice

Earnings

Cash

Save

Budget

Cost

Credit

Time

Live Life

life·style: *the way we live*

Lets start a new lifestyle.

One in which you will live within your means and save money. You will live and enjoy all that life has to offer.

You will pay attention to the way you feel and become aware of the purchases that you make. You will not spend money so that you can keep up with others.

You will pay attention to the retailers advertising and displays. Resist the temptation to purchase. You are aware of the fact that they spend a lot of money in advertising in an attempt to get your hard-earned money.

Do not make impulse buys. Take a 48-hour cooling down period before you make the purchase and only if it is a need.

You can have family nights, date nights and you can take turns with your family making different dishes or have your kids vote on their favorite meals.

Why not have movie nights with popcorn or games nights with snacks? Let's make it fun!

You will take a break from the restaurants and prepare your meals at home.

Your new motto will be "Less is More."

Only you can make it happen ...

be·hav·ior: *what a person does to make something change or to keep things the same*

It can take over two months before a new behavior become second nature. You have to change your habits, and this will not happen overnight.

You have to become aware of your thoughts and feelings when you are spending your money. Really focus on why you are buying things and determine how it makes you feel.

It may give you short-term satisfaction and you may end up paying over several times the value of the product or service that you are getting.

You need to factor this into the equation when purchasing something on credit because you would never purchase this if you were using cash at that price.

Separate your wants from your needs.

You will make mistakes along your path to transformation. Just forgive yourself and gain something from the experience. Then continue on with your journey.

You will not be defeated ...

sacrifice: give up or reduce something that you believe to be important

Yes,
you will have to make sacrifices
along the way. It will be extremely hard at first
but over time it will get easier.

Is that second vehicle really required? Do you
need this big house or apartment? Do you need to
go to those restaurants?

You have to determine the sacrifices that you
need to make.

Do not focus
on the things that you can't have but rather the
things that you can.

The things that we value in life are the
experiences that we have with our family and
friends. Let's make lots of happy memories.

The reward is near ...

in·come: *money that you receive*

How about
some additional income?
Can you consider picking up a side hustle?

Can you work extra hours
at your current job? How about picking
up a part time job for a while.?

There are multiple opportunities
available today as I know several people that are
working with one of the various delivery services.
Can you use your skills, talents or experiences to
pick up some work.

The extra cash
can go dircctly on your dcbt and or savings for
emergencies.

If you get any windfall of money, put it directly to
your debt or towards your savings.

Go hustle and get that income...

cash: *paper notes and coins*

Cash is awesome
and will allow you to commit to your budget. It allows you to truly realize how much services and products cost.

In today's society,
we are encouraged to use credit cards, debit cards, e-transfers, etc.

I love cash and you should as well.
It is still legal tender, and I would encourage you to use it.

You will definitely pay more attention to your purchases. Once you start using cash and get into the habit, it will become second nature.

You will not get into financial difficulty as you are living within your means.

Cash is golden ...

save: *putting money away for later*

Your new friend is Matic, and his first name is Auto. There is absolutely no charge for his services.

You can set up Auto Matic payments with your financial institute and have a fixed amount get deposited to a saving account.

This is critical as you need a backup plan with some cash available for when unexpected things occur.

I will guarantee that life does happen, and you will need some help for when an emergency occurs. You will be prepared, and it will eliminate any additional stress from not being ready.

If you want to experience financial security and build wealth, then you have to save money.

Once you have established some savings. You may even consider borrowing from yourself to throw a few dollars towards your debt as the intertest rate will be zero percent.

Save money and it will save you ...

TIP

$5 a day for 5 years @ 5 %
= over $10,000

$5 a day for 5 years @ 10% (average of stock market)
= almost $12,000

$5.25 a day for 33 years @ 10%
= over 1/2 Million Dollars

bud·get: keeping track of how much you have coming in and going out

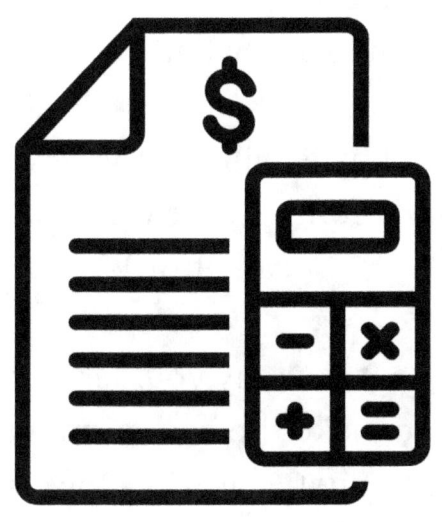

Creating a budget is a necessity.
You may feel that it is evil, but it isn't. It will make you accountable and prevent you from spending money that you do not have.

You can use sheets of paper, calendars, spreadsheets or free software. You just have to use something and whatever works for you.

This plan on a page will keep your expenses from getting out of control as it will tell you what you can afford.

Make sure that you pay yourself and your debts. You have to make the commitment to sticking with your budget as it will allow you financial freedom.

It's your journal to financial independence ...

cost: *amount that you pay to obtain something*

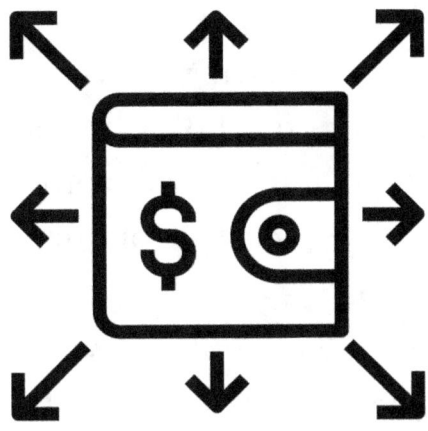

You have to reduce your costs. List all of your expenses from your coffee purchases to you mortgage payments.

Do you need; lunch & dinners at restaurants, a expensive car, a second vehicle, trips, etc.

Can you turn down your heat a little or your hot water boiler. Reduce your dryer usage and use the clothesline. Shop the flyers and use coupons for your groceries.

How about getting outside and enjoying mother nature and perhaps eliminating that fitness membership or that drive to the store.

You are the one that has to list all your monthly expenses and slash or eliminate them. I cannot tell you which ones to visit as this is something that you have to analyze for yourself.

The important thing is that you decrease your expenses. Stop purchasing wants and only purchase needs.

You got this ...

cred·it: getting goods, services or cash and agreeing to pay later

Do not use credit cards.

You have to plan for your financial freedom.

If you have credit card debt then it means that you could not afford the purchases or services that you made.

The interest charges on some of the cards are extremely high and can take you years to pay off.

Make contact with your card holder to see if you can get a rate reduction. The worst they can say is no.

You have to use the services from Auto Matic to assist you in getting out of debt. You have to make more than the minimum monthly payments.

It's not overly important
as to which cards that you pay off first. Some people will tell you to pay off the highest interest rate first. Others will tell you to pay off the lowest balance first. You just have to transfer the payment of any cards that are paid off to one of the others.

I will not tell you
to close your accounts or to cut up your cards. This is something that you can decide for yourself but will tell you to not use them anymore.

Do not spend what you do not have ...

T.I.P

Every $1000 in credit card debt @ 29.9% interest equals

Payment $10 or 3%
= 24 years and $4,655 in payments

Additional Payment $10 monthly
= 6 years & $1,922 in payments

Additional Payment $40 monthly
= 1 yr 11 months & almost $1297 in payments

time: period of action that is continuous

It will take some time
to eliminate your debt and to build your
savings fund.

The debt never occurred overnight,
and it cannot get resolved overnight as well.

You have to make a goal
for a certain time and monitor your progress
along the way.

You can decide
the timeframe for eliminating your debt. Be
realistic and set obtainable time frames.
Celebrate your victories along the way and pat
yourself on the back.

Success is near ...

live life: to do as much as you can or want

Live life in the present
but be prepared for the future.

Financial wealth
will bring you financial security.
There is enough stress in our everyday lives
without the need for financial stress.

Live within your means
and spend your hard-earned money wisely.

Living life to the fullest
is not about having nice expensive fancy material things.
It's about forming great lasting memories
and being surrounded by your
Family & Friends.

Live life to the fullest. You deserve It ...

You will have the freedom to do:

What you want,
When you want
How you want.

If you like the book, please leave some feedback.

Thank You !!!

www.ingramcontent.com/pod-product-compliance
Lightning Source LLC
Chambersburg PA
CBHW071148240526
45465CB00024D/W/2126